THE PISTOL IN WAR

THE PISTOL IN WAR

TRAINING WITH REVOLVER

and SELF-LOADING PISTOL

by

CAPTAIN E. H. ROBINSON

late R.A.F.

Winner H.M. The King's Prize, Bisley, 1923
Author of " Rifle and Ammunition,"
" Rifle and Target," etc.
Editor, " N.R.A. Journal "

ALDERSHOT

GALE & POLDEN LIMITED

PRINTED IN GREAT BRITAIN BY
GALE & POLDEN LIMITED
ALDERSHOT
—

1941

P-8801

FOREWORD

By Major-General Sir Alan Hunter,
K.C.V.O., C.B., C.M.G., D.S.O., M.C.

In the Army to-day, the majority of officers, and many men, are armed with the revolver for personal protection.

There are such a multitude of items which have to be learnt and practised that the military day, week and year seldom seem to be long enough to fit them all in.

In consequence, the degree of training of officers and men in the use of the revolver is reduced in practice to the lowest possible point compatible with safety to their comrades. In fact, the standard is often so low that this safety will also be conferred upon the enemy.

But in spite of the many hours spent in organized training, it will often be found possible to snatch a few moments for learning to handle the revolver with sufficient skill ; with the result that the individual concerned will become confident that, in emergency, he can defend himself effectively.

To these officers and men I recommend Captain Robinson's book. It has been specially designed to fill the needs of those who consider that if they are armed with a weapon, it is their own business to make themselves efficient in its use.

Alan Hunter.

CONTENTS

LIST OF PLATES

LIST OF DIAGRAMS

ACKNOWLEDGMENTS

No book has ever been written without the author receiving a great deal of help, consciously or unconsciously given and accepted. This small work is no exception.

My own indebtedness goes back to days before the Great War, when the late Mr. Maurice Blood, then a champion pistol shot, gave me much instruction. I also owe a great deal of my early knowledge to that extraordinary and vivid personality, the late Mr. Walter Winans. During the Great War I had many talks with Captain C. D. Tracy of the King's Own (Royal Lancaster) Regiment, who in 1917 and 1918 was in charge of the Southern Command Revolver School at Wareham.

In the actual preparation of this book I acknowledge with gratitude the help given me by Major-General Sir Alan Hunter and Captain T. S. Smith (winner of the King's Prize, 1939) by reading the proofs and script and making many valuable suggestions, all of which I have used.

Also I am indebted to Mr. Ernest Polden, a pistol shot of more than ordinary ability, for posing for, and directing the taking of, the photographs to illustrate particular points in the all-important matters of grip, trigger pressing and aiming. It should be noted that Mr. Polden was using for these photographs a Webley .38 inch revolver, which differs slightly in shape from the official Enfield pattern. The photographs are not the less useful on that account.

E. H. R.

PIRBRIGHT,
April 9th, 1940.

FIRST PRINCIPLES

THERE is one main principle of pistol shooting in war to which all training must lead. This is to secure a bullseye on the target in the shortest possible time after that target has been seen.

To this end what is known as " instinctive " shooting must be developed. This means that the pistol is directed, just as the finger is pointed without conscious aim taken over the sights.

Generally speaking, war shooting with a pistol is at short ranges and the sort of aiming which is done in slow-fire competition work is a waste of time.

Consider yourself as advancing around the traverse of a trench or looking round from the sheltered side of a derelict armoured fighting vehicle.

Your pistol is in your hand and your arm is in the " ready position "—that is, at an angle of about 45° from the vertical. The muzzle of the pistol is pointed in the general direction in which a possible enemy may appear.

You see the enemy. If you take conscious aim with the eye you will waste two or three or even more valuable seconds. On the other hand, if you come up and aim instinctively your shot will be away within one second. A skilled man will have

1

pulled the trigger within a fraction of a second of seeing the target.

The shot will be away even quicker if the pistol is fired from the hip.

Training in this method is devoted to making the pistol just as much a part of the hand as is the forefinger, in spite of the handicap imposed by the weight of the pistol and sometimes by the weight of the stock.

Make no mistake about it, this kind of dexterity is only obtained by a great deal of practice. Some men become efficient more quickly than others, but anyone can become a good pistol shot if he will devote sufficient time and thought to all the small details.

It is the object of this book to emphasize these details and to show how perfection can best be obtained. Nothing that is to be said here is intended to override the excellent official handbook, " Small Arms Training," Volume I, Pamphlet 11, nor will the book replace practice under a competent instructor.

The hints here given are intended as a supplement to the textbook and to instruction on the range.

The degree of efficiency laid down in " Small Arms Training " is the putting of a bullet into a rectangle 16 inches high by 12 inches wide at 10 yards in one second. To this I would add that this degree of proficiency should be obtained with either hand and from any position.

two

TYPES OF PISTOL

A LARGE number of men in the Fighting Forces
are now armed with what is familiarly known
as the " hand gun." It is officially issued to com-
batant officers in the Army, to officers and men in
the Royal Air Force, to officers and other ranks in
the Royal Armoured Corps and to the Military
Police. There is besides a very considerable issue
of revolvers in the Royal Navy.

At the time of writing there are three different
types of hand gun in use. There is the " Pistol
.38 inch," designed on behalf of the Government
by Webley & Scott, Ltd, which, it is understood, is
to be ultimately the official arm of all Services.
This is actually a revolver. There is also the .455
inch revolver and the Colt automatic .45 inch.

The figures indicate the " calibre " or nominal
diameter of the bore.

Other types may be in use or may be issued, but
the principles of using them are the same, particularly as regards instinctive shooting. The only
points to be remembered are that each type has its
own peculiarities and that the " feel " of the gun
must be learned thoroughly.

Preliminary training is often done with .22 inch
ammunition. This cheap and accurate cartridge

gives excellent preliminary practice, but it is a mistake to use a different type of gun for small-bore training. If you are armed with a .38 inch pistol the .22 arm you use for initial practice should be the .38 with a .22 attachment or with special chamber and barrel. The same remarks, of course, apply to the other types of hand gun.

There is one thing that should be remembered with regard to small-bore practice. The .22 cartridge gives practically no recoil whereas the recoil of the full-charge cartridge is fairly heavy. It is well, therefore, not to mix the two types of practice. When you get through your preliminary .22 work leave that cartridge unless things are going wrong and you feel the need for an elementary refresher course. When you are thoroughly proficient you will probably find yourself able to switch from full bore to small bore and back again without trouble, but whilst you are learning, changing about will only lead to trouble and probably delay the attainment of efficiency.

three

SAFETY PRECAUTIONS

B ECAUSE of its short barrel the pistol is a dangerous weapon when loaded and in the hands of an inexpert man.

For this reason certain very rigid rules must be laid down for its use.

The first of these is that whenever you take a pistol into your hand you should " prove " it. That is, you should open the action to see that there is no round in the cylinder. In the case of the automatic it is necessary to see that there is not a loaded magazine in place and that there is no round in the chamber.

The pistol should be proved always, except on actual active service, when you take it from the holster, when you pick it up from the table or when it is handed to you by someone else, even if it is a senior officer and he tells you it is not loaded. Never believe anything except the evidence of your own eyes.

Certain other safety precautions are laid down in " Small Arms Training." These govern the " ready position " which differs for unmounted and mounted troops and to some extent for the crews of armoured fighting vehicles. They are impressed by instructors over and over again during the course and should never be neglected.

Mainly these rules are concerned with seeing that the pistol is only loaded when the student is facing the target and about to fire, and that when it is loaded it is held in such a position that should it go off accidentally it will damage neither the firer nor his friends.

Never neglect the safety precautions.

Never, until you are about to go into battle, load the pistol away from a range, not even to show " how it is done."

There is another series of safety precautions to be observed before and during battle.

First of all, make sure that your pistol is loaded.

The second is to reload the instant you think you have finished and always when opportunity offers.

The third is never to advance with only two or three unfired rounds in the chamber or magazine.

And the fourth is when advancing round cover always hold your pistol in your outside hand.

four

ACCURACY

IN war shooting the pistol has usually to contend with a large target. Generally it will be the body of a man—upright—which may be taken as a rectangle 16 inches high by 12 inches wide.

A hit anywhere within this rectangle can be reckoned to strike a vital part and give a " knock-out." But the nearer the hit is to the centre the more certain is the knock-out.

To hit such a target, aiming instinctively, at 10 yards should be fairly easy. As has already been said, an efficient shot should be able to put one bullet into such a rectangle in one second.

At 20 yards this target is twice as difficult to hit as it is at 10 yards.

At 50 yards it is five times as difficult to hit as at 10 yards.

The difficulty of hitting a target of a given size at a longer range is self-evident. It can be appreciated fully when the marksman has some knowledge of " angular measurement."

Angular measurement is always used by gunners and is also used by expert marksmen—the kind that go in for sniping.

In angular measurement a full circle is divided

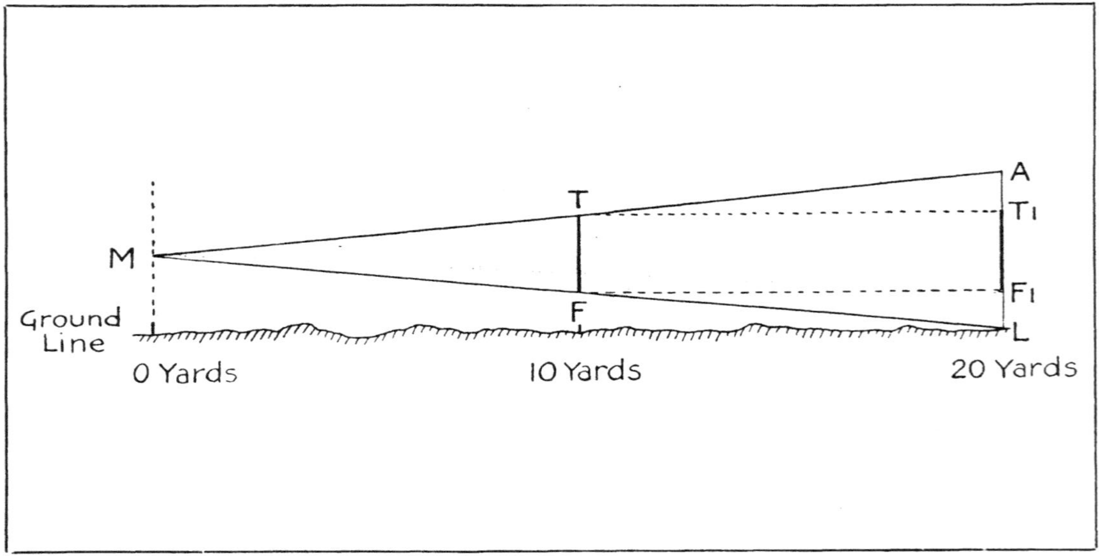

FIG. 1.—ILLUSTRATING "ANGULAR MEASUREMENT."

The line T_1F_1 subtends only half the angle of TF, though both are of the same physical dimensions. See text for explanation.

into 360 degrees (°). Each degree is further divided into 60 minutes (').

A quarter of a circle—a right angle when lines are drawn from the centre to the circumference—contains 90°.

No matter how large the circle it contains 360° and the quarter circle 90°.

It follows that two lines drawn at an angle to one another, no matter how long they are, will always " subtend the same angle."

Consider the diagram (Fig. 1). The two lines MA and ML are drawn at an angle starting from the muzzle of the pistol M. Suppose it is an angle of 2°. The line TF, which represents a target 10 yards from the muzzle, subtends 2°. So, also, does the line AL which is twice the distance from the muzzle—20 yards.

See what follows. If the line TF represents our target it subtends 2° of angle at 10 yards. Now move that target back to 20 yards. It is now represented by the line T_1F_1. That line subtends only 1° of angle at 20 yards. Therefore it is twice as difficult to hit.

This brings us to another important point on which we have to think. Dispersal of fire.

A rifle, even a short-barrelled rifle like the pistol, is an accurate arm, but, except by accident, it is not capable of putting two shots through the same hole at, say, 10 yards.

Each bullet is likely to weigh slightly more or less than another. Each cartridge is likely to have a little more or a little less powder than its neighbour in the cylinder or magazine. Therefore no two

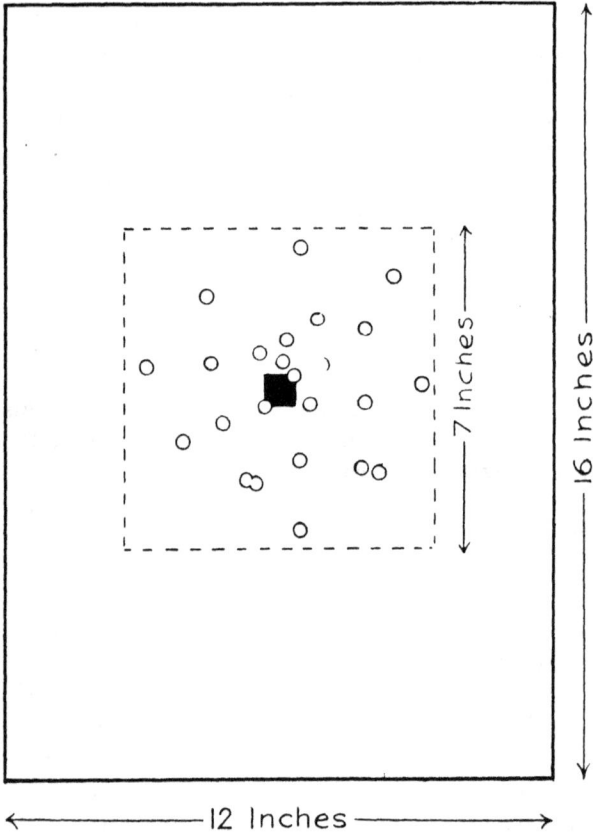

FIG. 2.—24 Shots fired from a Rest with .38 inch
Pistol at 50 Yards.

The normal 12 inches by 16 inches test target has been
drawn round the group.   Compare with Fig. 3, p. 12.

bullets will have exactly the same velocity—except by accident.

If the pistol is fired from a rigid rest, so that it is aimed at exactly the same place for each shot, the bullets will be found to hit the target so as to form a more or less circular group. The size of this circle is a measure of the accuracy of the pistol and its ammunition (Fig. 2).

Continue firing from the rest and the size of the group will enlarge a little but the majority of the bullets will still be hitting within the original circle.

If you continue shooting from the rest for a considerable number of rounds you will see that most of the bullets have hit near the centre of the group. Eventually the target at the centre of the group will be shot clean away.

It is possible to calculate, from any given size of group, how many shots out of 100 or 1,000 will be found within a circle half or a quarter or a tenth of the diameter of the whole group. This is a fascinating subject but outside the theme of this work. If you are interested you will find the whole subject dealt with in Part III, Chapter VIII, of " The Textbook of Small Arms (1929)," page 352.

Look again at Fig. 1 and see where these considerations lead us.

When we shoot from the hand we add our own " personal error " to that of the pistol. The group we make is bigger than that which could be made from the rest. The size of the group is now a measure of our own capabilities.

Suppose the line *TF* on the figure represents an

11

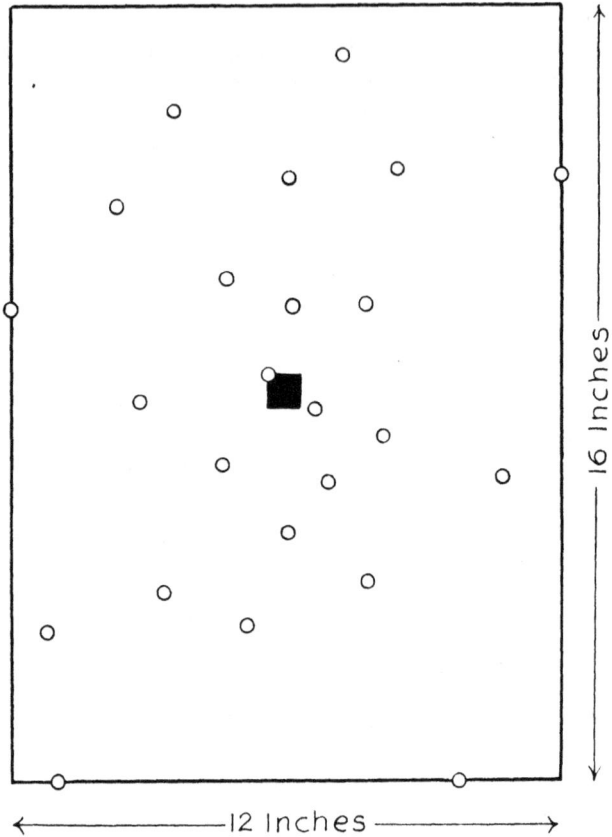

16 Inches

12 Inches

Fig. 3.—24 Shots fired by a Skilled Military Instructor, using .38 inch Pistol at 10 Yards.

Single action. Average time for each group of six shots just under 6 seconds. Five minutes' rest between each group of six. Position " off hand."

edgeways view of a target which we can just manage to hit with all our shots at 10 yards.

The two lines MA and ML now represent a lengthways section through a cone which contains all the shots fired.

The edgeways section through the cone shown at the line TF is the circular group containing all our shots.

Move the target back to T_1F_1 at 20 yards and it is manifest that a number of our shots will be scattered round the edges of the target.

We have already stated that the target is twice as difficult to hit when it is placed twice the distance away. Also we have learned that the majority of our shots tend to hit the centre of the target. It would seem, therefore, that the target at 20 yards would not be quite twice as difficult to hit as one at 10 yards.

This is true if we go on shooting for an infinite, or at any rate, a very large, number of rounds.

In practice we only shoot six rounds in one group. In war we may only get the chance of getting away one round.

Practically, therefore, it is true to say that if you double the distance of the target you halve your chance of hitting it.

Revolver ammunition is not as accurate as that made for the rifle. There is no need that it should be. All that is necessary is that it should group more closely than a skilled man can hold for competition purposes and that it should hit a large mark with certainty at short range, when properly fired, for war purposes.

The .455 revolver cartridge should group inside 8 inches at 50 yards.

The .38 pistol cartridge should group within 7 inches at 50 yards. (See Fig. 2.)

These figures represent groups smaller than the average good man can make at that range, shooting without a rest. (See Fig. 3.)

It is interesting to remember, however, that the competition target used at Bisley before 1915 had a 4 inch bullseye at 50 yards and that one or two scores of 40 and 41 points out of 42 were usually made each year. These prize-winners were "experts" and were probably using specially selected ammunition. The same standard of long-range deliberate shooting could doubtless be obtained to-day if there were men able and willing to use the revolver for a purpose for which it was never intended.

Deliberate shooting with revolver and pistol has a considerable vogue in the United States. With the .22 cartridge it has some followers in this country. The National Rifle Association is still running postal matches for .22 pistol enthusiasts and a good many men at home stations find time to indulge in it.

five

THE GUN IN YOUR HAND

WHEN you start pistol shooting you must think carefully about every action.

You have to think, and look, to make sure that you are gripping properly. You have to think whether your finger is on the trigger in the proper position, and you have to think really hard about the very important business of trigger pressing.

A proper grip and proper trigger pressing are essentials to good shooting.

If we had to think about them every time we fired pistol shooting would be a very slow game.

Luckily our muscles can " remember " just as well as our brains. By constant drill the muscles of the hand can be trained to take the proper grip and to press the trigger correctly. Also the muscles of the wrist and arm can be trained to offer the correct resistance to the recoil, at just the right moment and without waste of effort. At first these things will seem difficult. Then, at first slowly and then more rapidly, the muscles seem to know what is required of them. Without conscious thought on our part they take up their proper position.

When that stage is reached we only think if something is wrong. If we have taken up a strange gun, for instance, or if there is a lump of mud on the butt or a bruise or blister on palm or fingers.

15

six

THE GRIP

THE first essential of good shooting with the hand gun is the cultivation of the proper grip. The expert grips consistently but not very hard.

Take the butt in your hand so that the joint of the middle finger next to the knuckle is right up between the trigger guard and the butt with the third and little fingers close to it and all three fingers pressing the butt into the palm of the hand. (See Plate I.)

This brings the index finger in a position to coil snugly around the trigger and the correct grip is such that the index finger is curled round the lower rather than the upper part of the trigger so that the most efficient leverage can be exerted.

The position of the thumb is important. It differs with different "guns." With the .38 pistol the thumb is curled over towards the knuckle of the second finger. With the .455 revolver it may be fully extended and the inside should make a firm contact with the top of the shoulder of the butt. It is important that the tip of the thumb should not touch any part of the pistol.

The bruised thumb tip which results from having it in contact with the frame or the cylinder catch at the moment of firing is usually quite a sufficient lesson for the man who gets his thumb in the wrong position.

Once the correct grip is obtained great pains should be taken to make sure that it is never altered. In other words, make muscular memory perfect by drill and practice.

The great thing is to be able to take the proper grip by sense of touch. The fingers should close round the butt and take up the correct position without any conscious effort just as the fingers of an artist close on his pencil or brush or those of a bowler grip his ball.

Plate II is an awful example of how not to hold a pistol. Everything is wrong.

It is a good thing to practise taking the correct grip in the dark or with the hand hanging down and slightly behind the back or with the eyes closed.

The size of the hand in relation to the stock of the pistol has a considerable influence on the grip. Claims are made that the stock of the .38 pistol is of a better size to suit most men than that of the old .455. The .38 stock certainly suits the small-handed man better than that of the old Service revolver, but many men who have become used to the .455 complain that the .38 is too small.

It would seem a sensible thing to issue, say, three separate sizes of wood side-pieces for the stock so that a man can suit the grip to his hand, but this has not been done.

The Army Rifle Association and the National Rifle Association for competitions under their rules allow the stock to be bound with electricians' tape or some other material which will cause no actual damage.

Since a man's life may depend on his correct grip on his pistol butt in a sudden emergency there would seem to be no reason at all why he should not bind the stock so that it fits his hand. Unfortunately there is considerable official prejudice against any interference with Service arms and it is probable that any attempt at a proper fitting of the butt would lead to " trouble."

The grip on the butt of the automatic pistol is much the same as for the revolver. The great thing is that the butt should fit the hand. There is a curved portion at the top of the butt and the " crutch " of the thumb should come right up to the curve. With the Colt automatic the straight thumb grip is preferred by most experts, but this depends much upon the relative sizes of butt and hand.

seven

PRESSING THE TRIGGER

WITH the revolver (which includes the Pistol .38 inch) two separate methods of firing have to be learned.

Single Action.—In this the hammer is cocked with the thumb. Cocking the hammer rotates the cylinder and brings a fresh cartridge into position. When the hammer is held at full cock by the engagement of sear and bent in the trigger mechanism the thumb quickly takes up its normal position for firing. On pressing the trigger the hammer falls and the cartridge is fired.

Double Action.—The pull on the trigger is used to cock the hammer and rotate the cylinder. Pressure on the trigger is continued until the hammer falls and the cartridge is fired. The trigger is then immediately and fully released so that the process can be repeated to fire another shot.

With the automatic pistol, after the first shot, the recoil of the action throws out the spent case and, on the return of the action into position a fresh cartridge is fed into the chamber. It is only necessary to learn one method of trigger pressing with these pistols.

A description of the method of trigger pressing in

Single Action shooting will serve for the automatic pistol.

When Single Action trigger pressing has been mastered thoroughly the use of the Double Action method for quick shooting will be acquired without much trouble.

Directly he starts trigger pressing practice, using the Single Action method, the student will appreciate one of the reasons why it is necessary to learn the feel of the correct grip so that it is taken without conscious thought.

The first thing that has to be learned is to cock the hammer.

To do this, having first made sure that the pistol is empty, extend the arm fully, holding it at an angle of about 45° from the body, with the pistol pointing to the ground about three feet in front of you and in the direction of the target.

Shift your thumb up to cover the comb of the hammer. This cannot be done without shifting the grip slightly. The butt tends to come away from the palm of the hand and should be allowed to do so.

Draw the hammer back until it engages at full cock.

Do not touch the trigger whilst you are doing this. Let the back of your trigger finger touch lightly against the inside of the front part of the trigger guard.

Make sure that the grip is exactly restored to normal.

Raise the pistol to the level of the eye, looking at the mark but making no attempt to take an exact aim.

As the pistol comes up let the trigger finger start a slight pressure.

When you are quite sure you are ready squeeze on the trigger.

That word *squeeze* exactly describes the correct action. Imagine that you hold a small piece of sponge between your thumb and trigger finger and want to extract the last drop of moisture from it with one slow and definite action.

Note that though the thumb is mentioned as well as the trigger finger actually all the muscles of the hand are employed in the action.

You tighten the whole grip on the butt in the action of trigger pressing.

The first two or three times you try this you will probably pull the trigger right back so that it comes up against its stop with a bump. Learn to avoid this. Directly the hammer falls the trigger should be released fully.

Trigger pressing is a matter of touch and a sense of touch can be acquired only by constant practice.

It is well to get as much trigger pressing practice as possible before you fire your first round and since constant snapping of the hammer on an empty gun does not do it any good it is as well to acquire six " dummy " cartridges for work with the revolver. One will serve for automatic pistol work as unless there is a live round in the chamber the recoil action does not operate.

The student should here be warned that there are two schools of thought amongst pistol experts in this matter of trigger control.

One school says that the correct sense of touch

c

can be obtained only by concentrating on the trigger finger and nothing but the trigger finger.

The other school holds that the best way, at any rate for the beginner, is to concentrate on a squeeze between finger and thumb.

Though in rifle shooting I think with the first school, in pistol shooting I am with the second. I am quite sure that those who learn the thumb and finger squeeze method get better results in Double Action work.

eight

PRACTICE WITH THE TRIGGER

TRIGGER pressing practice and practice in taking the correct grip can go on side by side. The muscles of the hand will thus be educated in all the actions of firing.

At the same time the muscles of the arm and shoulder will be educated and exercised.

Do your practice with the full weight Service pistol.

Remember to keep the wrist taut and the forearm straight. The necessity for this does not appear until you fire the Service cartridge, but it is well to get into good habits from the start. (See Plate III.)

Watch the muzzle of the pistol each time you pull the trigger. Go on with your trigger pressing practice until there is no movement of the muzzle when the hammer falls.

If the muzzle moves appreciably as you move the trigger you are certainly pulling on the trigger instead of squeezing it.

A good way to correct any tendency to pull is to concentrate your mind on the pressure of the thumb rather than on that of the finger.

Do not forget the correct grip. The proper trigger squeeze is impossible if the grip is wrong.

nine

AIMING

BEFORE you can learn to shoot instinctively you must learn to aim consciously. But the practice you have already had in gripping and trigger pressing will have given your muscles some education in instinctive aiming.

Once you begin to grip and press the trigger properly you can start aiming practice with the empty gun. When you do so keep on thinking about grip and trigger pressing. You are now learning three things.

Aimed fire is part of the elementary work laid down in " Small Arms Training " and must be mastered.

The best elementary practice is to be had by aiming at your own eye reflected in a mirror about three yards away.

Practice 1.—Stand with the right shoulder towards the target (left shoulder if you are using the left hand).

The body and head should be upright and the legs placed so that the feet are about a pace apart. Toes of forward foot pointing towards target. Rear foot to the left of the line of fire and making an angle of about 90° with it.   (See Fig. 4.)

The stance to be taken up is the natural one that gives the firmest and steadiest position.

Prove the pistol.

Make sure that grip is correct.

The arm to be used is at an angle of about 45° with the body, the muzzle of the pistol pointing at the ground about three or four feet in front of

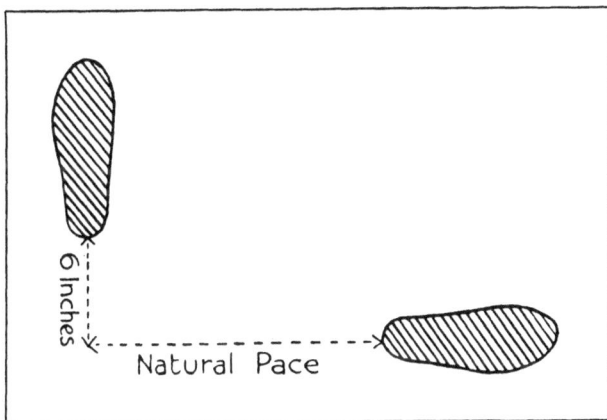

FIG. 4.—CORRECT POSITION OF FEET FOR " OFF HAND " STANCE.

the firer. The position of the wrist in this " ready position " is important. You should be able to see the whole of the top of the barrel when looking down at it.

Raise the pistol and aim over the sights, making sure that the foresight is in the centre of the backsight notch and that its tip is level with the shoulders of the backsight and that the sights are upright.

Do not press the trigger. Repeat the aiming practice several times until you understand what conscious aim means. After that you can forget the sights and give all your time to developing instinctive aim.

Practice 2.—Prove the pistol. Take up stance as for Practice 1. Make sure that grip is correct.

Raise the arm and, as you do so, start the squeeze on trigger. As the sights come to the level of your eye complete the squeeze so that the hammer falls.

The sights should not be deflected from the eye you aim at as the hammer falls.

Do this slowly at first, making sure that all actions are correct. Gradually speed up until you can get off an accurate shot, cocking hammer, raising arm and squeezing trigger, within one second.

Practice 3.—This is usually done with the instructor, but may be carried out with a fellow student.

Prove the pistol and show it, open, to instructor or companion who is helping.

Take up stance as for Practice 1. (The instructor will be about five yards away.) Go through all the motions of Practice 2, but aiming at instructor's eye. (See Plate IV.)

The standard required is that five out of six shots should be so directed as to have hit the instructor's face. The instructor will estimate the deflection. If you take the part of " target " yourself you will find that it is fairly easy to judge whether your face would have been hit.

Practice 4.—Place on the wall a good-sized mark. Say a two-inch black circle if you can stand four yards from it. Smaller if the distance is less. Take up stance as for Practice 2. Look at the mark. Close both eyes. Come up with the pistol pointing as nearly as you know to where you saw the mark. Then open the eyes and see how nearly you have obtained a correct aim.

Quite considerable accuracy in this " blindfold " shooting can be attained. It is very useful in developing instinctive or " sense of direction " aiming, and is most useful as a preliminary to night firing.

When you can point correctly three times out of five with the eyes shut try pressing the trigger before opening eyes.

ten

THE EYE AND AIMING

M OST men have one eye stronger than the other. With the majority the right is the " Master Eye." They shoot naturally from the right shoulder with the rifle and with the right hand with the pistol.

An important part of preliminary instruction in instinctive aiming is to throw up the arm and point, as rapidly as possible, at the instructor's eye.

This practice shows at once which is the master eye. You can try it for yourself.

Choose some prominent object three or four yards from you. Throw up your arm and point straight at it with the index finger.

Now cover the eye farthest from the arm you have thrown up. If you are using your master eye your aiming finger will still be seen covering the object at which you are pointing.

Repeat the pointing action with the other arm. Suppose you are now using your left arm. Cover the right eye and if your right eye is strongly the master you will see your finger pointing slightly to the right of the object.

Your master eye has tried to take control and you have not pointed quite straight.

Cover the right eye and repeat, the left hand

pointing. You are now aiming correctly. But if you uncover your right eye you will seem to be pointing to the left of the object.

By means of these experiments find out for yourself which is your master eye and the extent of your personal error.

Because one eye is usually the master, you are told to close the " disengaged " eye when firing.

Many men find it difficult to close the master eye and keep the other open. In some cases it is impossible.

A man who cannot close his master eye finds it difficult to shoot well with either hand, as he should be able to do. His only remedy for his disability is to find out exactly how far to the right he points when shooting with the left hand and a right master eye, or how far to the left he points when shooting with the right hand and a left master eye.

He must then teach himself to point instinctively to left or right of the target to compensate for his personal error.

eleven

WITH EITHER HAND

A S when you are advancing round cover in war it is necessary for your own safety that the pistol should be held in the outer hand, that is, the one not obstructed by the cover, you must learn to shoot with either hand.

A right-handed man will find that his left hand wants considerable training, but the main difficulty is not so much muscle education as aiming, which has already been mentioned.

Nevertheless, a great deal of work must be done to perfect grip and trigger pressing and the sooner it starts the better.

Directly the student is reasonably sure that he is doing the right thing with his natural hand he should start work with his other.

Everything is done exactly as before except that in the directions you read right for left and left for right.

twelve

DOUBLE ACTION

DOUBLE Action shooting, when the pull on the trigger is used to cock the hammer and revolve the cylinder, is more difficult than Single Action shooting.

The heavy and sustained pull on the trigger is likely to shift the grip unless the hold is good and the " squeeze " on the trigger has been thoroughly mastered.

The shifting of the grip means inaccurate shooting. Usually shots fired with the right hand will tend to be high and to the left if the grip has shifted. For this reason the Single Action method should always be used when possible. (See Plate IX.)

Double Action should be reserved for occasions when extreme speed is necessary, say in dealing with one or more enemies. When you need to use the Double Action you need it very much indeed.

Generally Single Action will be used at all ranges over 8 yards and Double Action reserved for really close work.

You may have no time to use the arm fully extended. The shot may have to be made from the hip or with arm half extended.

Put in all the time you can with the Double Action method. The empty gun exercises are

31

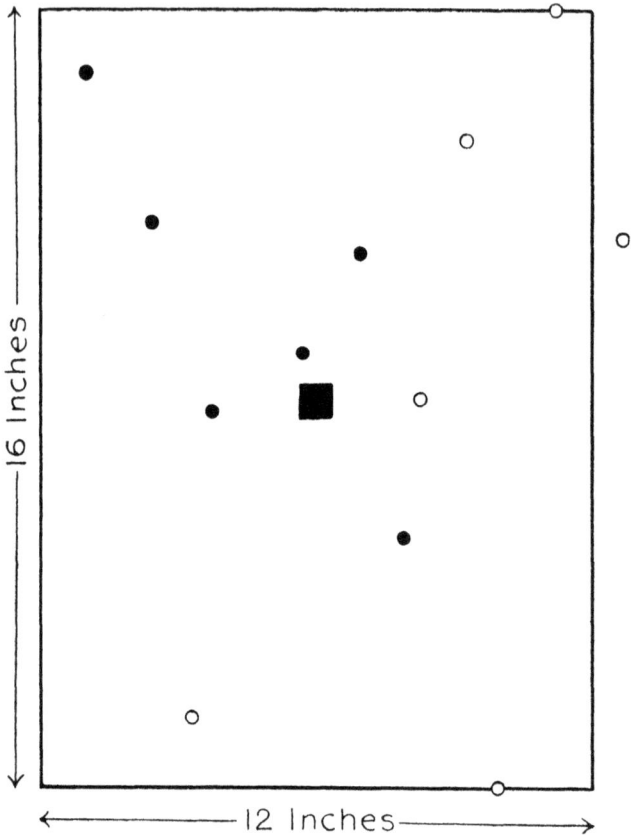

FIG. 5.—BLACK CIRCLES: SIX SHOTS IN 5 SECONDS, DOUBLE ACTION WITH RIGHT HAND. PLAIN CIRCLES: SIX SHOTS IN 6.25 SECONDS, DOUBLE ACTION WITH LEFT HAND.

Both fired by the same military instructor. Two targets used. Rest between groups only that required to reload chambers.

exactly the same as for Single Action with the exception that the thumb is not used to cock the hammer.

If you have learned to squeeze the trigger properly between thumb and finger in Single Action work you should have little difficulty in getting your shots away with fair accuracy. After some work with the extended arm, try hip shooting.

Look at the spot you wish to hit—the middle of the target—and you will be surprised to find that shooting from the hip is nearly as accurate as shooting with arm extended so that the pistol is at eye-level.

Practise hip shooting with an instructor or friend, taking care, of course, to prove the pistol before getting to work.

Two or three friends working together can get useful practice in rapid Double Action shooting at two or more enemies.

Unless Double Action shooting is more rapid than the Single Action method it is useless to worry with it. Therefore speed with accuracy must be the result of your drill.

Watch for the fault of poking the muzzle of the pistol down. A loose wrist or a badly shifted grip often results in this error.

Do not forget that your own life and the lives of others may depend on your ability to use the Double Action effectively. Therefore do not grudge the time spent in overcoming its many difficulties.

And learn to use the pistol from any position.

thirteen

BOTH EYES OPEN

THE really expert war pistol shot always keeps
both eyes open, however much his instructors
may have insisted on the necessity of closing the eye
farthest from the target.

In the section on aiming something has been said
about the difficulty which some men find in closing
the master eye. This is not the major reason for
keeping both eyes open when in action.

If you close one eye you cut out a quarter to a
third of your all-round vision. The amount you
cut out depends on how your eyes are set in your
head. A good all-round view may be of the
utmost importance.

Should your master eye be strongly the master
you will find no difficulty at all in shooting with both
eyes open when your master eye is the right one and
you are using your right hand—or the reverse.

Two-eyed shooting when using the other hand
depends on a knowledge and mastery of the error
introduced by letting, say, the right eye govern a
left-hand shot. Here again drill and drill and yet
more drill is the way to overcome the difficulty.
But do not attempt two-eyed shooting until you
have mastered one-eyed marksmanship. If, however, you have the disability already mentioned
you must practise it from the first.

34

fourteen

ON THE RANGE

L ONG before you have reached the degree of efficiency to which these notes have led you it is to be supposed that you will have been introduced to the range and will have had some actual shooting.

Presumably your breaking-in will have been gradual. You will have started with the .22 cartridge and will have found little difference from working with the empty pistol, except that you have the satisfaction, or disappointment, of seeing the actual strike of the bullet on the target.

Now is the time to remember all you have learned in your work with the empty gun. You should have a very good idea of the reason for any errors that appear and should know how to correct them.

Faulty trigger squeezing and faulty grip are the cause of most bad shots though, of course, you may not have pointed the pistol properly.

Try to put all your shots in the very centre of the target. Time spent in learning accuracy with the very accurate .22 cartridge, and in learning to direct your shots centrally when there is no recoil to shift your grip and tire your wrist, is time very well spent indeed.

If you cannot shoot well with the .22 you certainly will not shoot well with the full bore.

Try to imagine that your arm is a solid piece of wood, rigidly attached to the pistol, pivoted at the shoulder and with only the trigger finger and thumb and to a small extent the other fingers, free to make any movement.* This hint should have been given at the very beginning of the book, but has been reserved until now for additional emphasis and because you will find out its value directly you start work with the full-charge cartridge. (See Plates III, V, VI and VII.)

 Besides good squeeze and grip the rigid wrist is essential to accuracy and a rigid wrist is hardly possible without a rigid arm behind it.

By this time you should have found out that it is not necessary to lower the arm to the full 45° to cock the hammer. A very little lowering of the arm is all that is necessary for the thumb to work the hammer smoothly. In this way speed is attained in the Single Action method.

All preliminary range work is done " off hand," that is, with the arm fully extended, coming up from the ready position when the word " go " is given.

Preliminary work should be done Single Action for reasons that will be evident from what has already been said.

---

* It has been pointed out that there are two schools of thought about this "wooden arm" idea. If too much insisted upon it may lead to too tight a grip being taken—a very serious fault. I am told that exponents of the "wooden arm" never practise what they preach. A certain degree of rigidity is necessary but it must not be taken too far.

In loading the pistol do so according to the official instructions as laid down in the training manual, but endeavour to learn as quickly as possible to place the cartridges in the chambers of the cylinder two at a time. If you use the thumb and first two fingers to grip the cartridges by their bases you will soon learn how to pick them up exactly the right distance apart so that they go home into the chamber smartly. (See Plate VIII.)

From time to time revolver loading clips have been put on the market, but according to " The Textbook of Small Arms (1929)," they have never been successful. I had some in 1912, but discarded them for many good and sufficient reasons.

One or more loaded magazines will be carried for the automatic pistol and reloaded as occasion requires.

The chief difficulty about full-charge shooting is that the recoil tends to shift the grip. If the grip does shift try to correct it when recocking the hammer. If you cannot do this the only expedient is to know the error you may expect from the shift and point the pistol accordingly when firing. (See Plate IX.)

Experiments can be carried out with bad and good grips using the small-bore cartridge. This will give some idea of the error to be expected. But remember that your shooting with the full-charge cartridge will be different to an extent which you can only find out by further experiment on the range.

Lucky is the man who is stationed near a fully equipped pistol range and has the opportunity to use it.

D

He will then be able to have experience with moving and bobbing targets, targets which appear suddenly and those which appear in unexpected places as in a trench constructed to give exercise in " mopping up " operations.

Sense of direction is the only method that can be used at bobbing and unexpected targets and as these are by far the most likely to be encountered in war the sense-of-direction aim has to be cultivated from the first.

With targets moving across a front aim must be taken in front and the pistol kept moving with the target just as the swing of a shot-gun is kept up. The swing should be from the waist and not from the shoulder. The distance in front will depend on the range and the speed of the target. Usually it will be necessary only to point the pistol just in front of the normal aiming mark.

Bobbing targets are usually exposed for a very short time and often from different parts of the stop butt for each succeeding exposure. They are good fun and excellent for cultivating speed with accuracy.

When working through a trench be ready for targets appearing simultaneously or in rapid succession. The Double Action may have to be used when you least expect it, but if you have the chance always cock the hammer with the thumb.

The men who design these trenches are full of invention. They want to test you fully as a war shot.

In one trench I went through in 1917 a figure appeared from a hole in the wall of the trench almost at my feet and when I was nearly on top of him. I missed and was told I was dead.

And because you have been through a trench once, do not expect to find the targets in the same place the next time you make the journey. You can be fairly sure that they will have been changed.

When you have finished firing clean your pistol as soon as possible. Clean from the breech if possible and do not forget the cylinder and chambers.

In cleaning an automatic pistol look particularly for unburnt grains of powder in the sliding parts of the action. The pistol cartridge has been much improved since 1914-18, but unburnt grains of powder are still a cause of jams if they are allowed to accumulate.

fifteen

LOWERING THE HAMMER

IF the gun has been cocked and the revolver has not been fired the hammer should be lowered before the gun is restored to the holster.

To do this take a good grip on the butt and place the thumb firmly on the hammer. Then, with the pistol pointing to the front and towards the ground about three feet away from the feet, press the trigger and lower the hammer gently keeping firm control throughout.

Do this many times with the empty gun before you attempt it with charged cylinder.

If the thumb is placed sideways on the hammer good control is obtained and the fingers alone are concerned with the grip on the butt.

Lowering the hammer brings the striker down on the cartridge that would have been fired. Recocking moves this cartridge on and if you do not remember this you may find yourself in the awkward predicament of pulling the trigger with an empty shell under the hammer.

It is very important to remember how many loaded cartridges remain to be used. As has previously been said, it is also important, in war, to reload at every opportunity.

If you have lowered the hammer on an unfired

round it is advisable to restore the cylinder to its normal position as soon as possible.

Many tricks, some of them almost sleight-of-hand—have been described for doing this without " breaking " the action. Actually the best way is to break the action and turn the cylinder so that the fired and unfired cases can be seen. If there is time replace empty cases with loaded ones. If not quickly revolve cylinder so that charged round on which hammer has been lowered comes next into position when the hammer is cocked. This is also the safest method in every way.

Do this many times using dummy cartridges before you attempt it with live rounds. Mark one of the dummy cartridges with a piece of stamp-paper on the base, so that you can see what you are doing when you move the cylinder.

Whilst on this subject it is well to point out that revolvers with a " break-down " action, such as the Webley and the Pistol .38, should never be opened nor closed with the hammer at full cock. This is liable to injure the mechanism. Besides which, closing the action with the hammer at full cock is distinctly dangerous.

sixteen

STOPPING POWER

THE pistol being a close-range arm, stopping power is important. If an enemy is close enough to you to enable a pistol to be used he must be stopped at once.

Stopping power is usually measured in terms of Striking Energy and it has been stated that a striking energy as low as 60 ft./lbs. is sufficient to stop a man.

But Striking Energy is not the whole of the story, as can be shown by a reference to the history of the rifle.

The .45 inch bullet of the old Martini-Henry rifle was a fine man-stopper. Its striking energy at 200 yards was about 1,200 ft./lbs. When our army changed over to the blunt-nosed .303 inch bullet, which had a striking energy of 1,380 ft./lbs. at 200 yards, the new bullet was found to be deficient in stopping power. Savage warriors failed to be impressed by the addition of 180 ft./lbs. of energy.

Good stopping power in the .303 inch projectile was not restored until the adoption of the pointed bullet. True, the striking energy of the Mark VII bullet is about 1,655 ft./lbs. at 200 yards, but the stopping power seems to depend more on the fact that the base-heavy bullet tends to turn over on impact than on the additional striking energy.

The .455 revolver bullet is known to be a very good man-stopper. At 10 yards its striking energy is about 210 ft./lbs. and it delivers a true knock-down blow when it hits on the body at anything up to 25 yards.

Many men who are now armed with the .38 inch pistol have the idea that because the bullet has a less diameter and less sectional density (weight, in pounds, divided by the square of the diameter in inches) it will have less stopping power.

Both bullets are made of lead and blunt-nosed lead bullets tend to set-up or mushroom on impact. Part of their stopping power can be attributed to this.*

At 10 yards the striking energy of the .38 inch pistol bullet is about 155 ft./lbs.

Within reason, stopping power depends on weight of projectile more than on velocity. For equal striking energy a heavy bullet with low velocity is a better man-stopper than a light bullet with high velocity. This is true for velocities up to 3,000 feet a second.

Arguing that high velocity is important—the weight of the bullet in pounds is multiplied by the square of the velocity in calculating striking energy —many men swear by the automatic pistol.

For instance, the Colt .45 inch automatic has a higher velocity than the .455 inch revolver and the

* A jacketed bullet for the .38 pistol has been experimented with. Those who have shot it at Bisley say that it lacks accuracy besides being suspect in the matter of stopping power.

striking energy of the bullet at 10 yards is 326 ft./lbs. This high striking energy looks very attractive, on paper.

Actually, the Colt .45 bullet is known to be a less efficient man-stopper than the .455 revolver bullet. It is probably less efficient than the bullet of the .38 pistol.

For reasons connected with the form of the mechanism, bullets for automatics are "compound," that is, they have a cupro-nickel envelope filled with a lead core. These hard-jacketed bullets do not readily deform or set up on impact. Unless they strike hard substance their energy is expended on clean penetration with comparatively small shock effect.

PLATE X

THE .38 REVOLVER.
The New Service Hand Gun.

seventeen

THE .38 PISTOL

THE new Service revolver, known officially as Pistol, Mk. I (.38 inch), is now coming into general use.

In appearance and action the new weapon is similar to, but smaller than, the regulation .455. It is remarkably handy, and the stock is well designed so that it gives a convenient grip and allows of a hold as high as possible in relation to the bore of the barrel. The consequence is that the weapon can be pointed much more easily than the old revolver. The sides of the stock are of walnut, and the convex metal surface at the back has a series of fine lateral ribs to improve the holding. (See Fig. 6, and Plate X opposite.)

The following brief particulars are published by permission of the War Office :—

BARREL WITH FORESIGHT.—The barrel is 5 inches long and has an actual bore of .352 inch, as shown in the table following this description. The dimension .38 inch is the nominal bullet diameter of the standard cartridge for which the pistol is made, and the pistol is so entitled in order to identify it with this ammunition. The foresight has a more prominent blade and the lower face of the blade is undercut to improve definition.

45

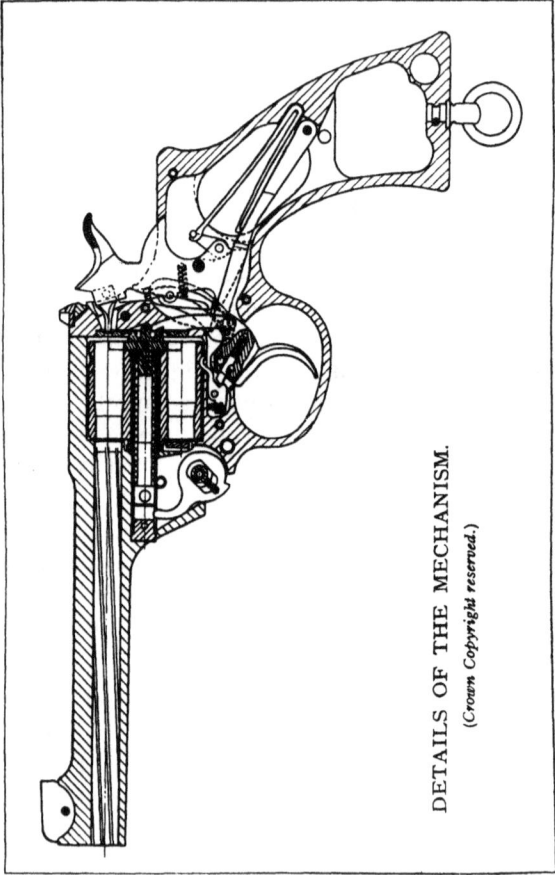

FIG. 6.

DETAILS OF THE MECHANISM.

(*Crown Copyright reserved.*)

BACKSIGHT.—This is formed as a rectangular notch with rounded corners at the top. In the case of early production, the notch is cut in a blade housed in a lateral groove in the upper end of the barrel catch and secured by two pins. The normal position of the blade is central, but blades offset to the extent of .02 inch right and left respectively are fitted as necessary to permit of adjustment when the pistols are shot for accuracy at the factory. In later production, the notch is cut centrally in the barrel catch, and foresight blades offset by a similar amount are fitted as necessary.

BODY.—A cover plate is fitted to the left side of the frame and secured by four screws. It is bored from the inside face to receive the left-hand portion of the axis pins for the hammer, trigger and cylinder stop, and the inside face is recessed to clear the cylinder pawl and the mainspring lever.

PAWL.—The pawl has two driving points for rotating the cylinder—the upper end and a step ; the former, acting on a tooth of the ratchet of the extractor, performs the first and major portion of the turning movement, and the step engaging the following tooth of the ratchet completes the movement and prevents anti-clockwise movement of the cylinder.

STOP, CYLINDER.—The stop engages the appropriate groove in the cylinder to prevent the latter from overturning in a clockwise direction. The acting rear end of the stop is pressed upward to the cylinder by a spiral spring which acts on the front end, so turning it about its axis. It is withdrawn from engagement, when the trigger is pressed, by a small trip pawl located with its spiral spring in the front of the trigger.

HAMMER.—Is fitted with a detachable striker having limited vertical movement on an axis pin.

STOP, SAFETY.—This component ensures that the hammer, when in the rebound position, cannot be driven forward by an accidental blow on the end of the thumbpiece. The stop is connected at its lower end to, and operated by, the trigger, its upper end being interposed between the front of the hammer and the body as the hammer moves back into the rebound position.

MARKING.—The pistol is marked for identification with the place and year of manufacture, " Crown " and " No. 2, Mk. I," on the right side of the body, and " Cal. .38 " on the upper surface of the barrel. The series number is marked on the front of the barrel and body near the joint, and on the rear end of the cylinder.

All component parts are special to the pistol.

The weight and overall dimensions and other general particulars are as follows :—

Weight : 1 lb. 11½ oz.
Length : 10¼ inches.
Length (diagonally) : 11¼ inches.
Depth : 5 inches.
Number of chambers : 6.
Bore : .352 inch.
Rifling :—
  Number of grooves : 7.
  Direction : R.H.

Pitch : One turn in 15 inches or 42.61 calibres.
Form : Concentric.
Width of grooves : .125 inch.
Depth of grooves : .005 inch.

Pull-off :—

Single Action : 5 to 6 lbs.
Double Action : 13 to 15 lbs.

CARTRIDGE, S.A., BALL, REVOLVER, .380 INCH.—
The Cartridge consists of a case with percussion cap,
charge and bullet.

The *case* is made of solid drawn brass.

The *percussion cap* is made of brass and contains
from .2 to .3 grains of cap composition covered with
a tinfoil disc.

The *charge* consists of about 4 grains of cordite.

The *bullet*, which weighs 200 grains, is made of
lead alloy, and has two cannelures formed round
the body filled with a beeswax lubricant.

The bullet is secured to the case by a small rolled
cannelure in the latter and by slightly coning the
mouth of the case on to the bullet.

Marking on the base consists of :—

(*a*) The calibre.
(*b*) The contractor's initials or recognized trade
mark ; and
(*c*) The year of manufacture.

Overall length of cartridge : 1.245 inch.
Total weight of cartridge : Approx. 266 grains.
Mean O.V. at 30 feet from muzzle : 590 ft./sec.
Mean pressure : 7 tons per sq. inch.
Figure of merit at 50 yards range : 3.5 inch.

eighteen

THE WEBLEY REVOLVER, .455 INCH, MARK VI

THE general description of the .38 pistol will serve as a guide to the construction of the old Webley revolver.

The weight, overall dimensions and other particulars are as follows :—

Weight : 2 lb. 4 oz.

Length : 11¼ inches.

Number of chambers : 6.

Length of barrel : 6 inches.

Number of grooves : 7.

Bore : .455 inch.

Cartridge, S.A., Ball, Revolver : .455 inch.

Bullet : Weight, 265 grains ; 3 cannelures, lubricated with beeswax ; round nose and hollow base ; lead alloy.

Case : Solid drawn brass.

Charge : About 5½ grains chopped cordite.

Mean O.V. at 30 feet from muzzle : 580 feet per second.

Mean pressure : 5½ tons per square inch.

Figure of merit at 50 yards range : 4 inches.

nineteen

THE COLT AUTOMATIC .45 INCH

"THE Colt is probably the most reliable of large-calibre self-loading pistols. The butt is correctly designed and slopes properly to the hand, the material is reliable and the workmanship accurate, parts are interchangeable and it will stand active service conditions fairly well." (The Textbook of Small Arms (1929), page 100.)

The recoil-operated action of the Colt is simple. The recoil following the discharge of the first cartridge drives back the slide. During the first part of the recoil action the barrel moves back with the slide, to which it is locked by lugs.

The backwards travel of the barrel is limited by a link on which it pivots. When this limit is reached the link pulls the barrel downwards, unlocking it from the slide.

The slide, to which the extractor is attached, continues its backwards movement, cocking the hammer, which is retained in the cocked position by the engagement of the sear with the bent.

The spent case is pressed against the ejector and flies out, to the right. The slide is then stopped by the recoil spring housing against which the return recoil spring has been compressed. The trigger

51

mechanism has also been disconnected by the movement of the slide so that the hammer cannot be released whilst the slide is in the backward position.

Meanwhile a fresh cartridge is being pressed upwards by the magazine spring and takes up its position between the slide and the chamber.

The recoil return spring now pushes the slide forward and the slide takes with it the new cartridge which is pushed into the chamber. The slide comes in contact with a lug on the upper part of the barrel, pushes the barrel forward and locks it into the recesses in the inner upward face of the slide.

Just as the forward movement is completed the trigger-locking mechanism is disengaged. This does not happen unless the action is completely closed. Thus it is impossible to fire with an unclosed action.

When the last cartridge in the magazine has been fired the magazine platform presses against, and lifts, a stop which holds the slide open.

When a fresh magazine is inserted the stop falls, the slide flies forward loading a new cartridge into the chamber and the pistol is ready to fire.

A safety catch is provided on the left-hand side, convenient for operation by the thumb in right-handed firing. There is also a " grip safety " on the butt. Unless the butt is firmly gripped the pistol cannot be fired. There is a half-cock notch on the hammer.

General particulars :—

Weight : 2 lb. 7 oz.

Length : 8½ inches.

Barrel length : 5 inches.

Cartridge :—

Bullet : Nickel-plated copper, or cupro-nickel envelope, with lead core ; weight, 224 grains.

Case : Solid drawn brass, rimless.

Charge : About 7 grains chopped cordite or equivalent nitro-cellulose.

Mean O.V. at 30 feet from muzzle : About 700 feet per second.

American-made cartridges are said to have an Observed Velocity at 25 feet from muzzle of 840 feet per second and a Striking Energy of 360 ft./lbs. at 8 yards range. These figures are for the usual round-nosed bullet fired from a 5-inch barrel. The standard United States bullet for the Colt Automatic, .45 inch, weighs 230 grains.

twenty

SOME HISTORY

THE user of a pistol or revolver, particularly when he has become expert, will be interested in the history of the arm. This book is therefore brought to a close with a brief account of the development of the " hand gun."

Revolving cannon—some of large calibre—are described in medieval manuscripts, but these bear little resemblance to that type of arm which has become known throughout the civilized world by the name of " revolver."

Before the introduction of the flint-lock, various revolving match-lock guns were in use. The earliest known in this country is an arquebus with four chambers, which is to be seen in the Tower of London collection and is supposed to have belonged to King Henry VIII. It appears to have been made in the first half of the sixteenth century.

Several similar weapons of a later date, of French and German manufacture, are to be found in the Paris Museum. In one a spring is attached to the barrel which engages in a stop in the chamber immediately it is in the proper position for firing. The chambers in all cases are moved round by hand. One has eight, another three, and the rest have five chambers.

In one arquebus of the middle of the seventeenth

century, the fire is communicated to the chambers by one flashpan only, which required repriming after each discharge.

A German double-chambered revolving gun made before 1650 is unique in principle. It has ten chambers, each long enough to contain two charges, one in front of the other, and fired by separate touch-holes. This allowed two shots to be fired in very quick succession. As the touch-holes were not covered, it was necessary to prime afresh each time the chamber was partly revolved. It is likely that the two charges sometimes went off together.

In the Birmingham Museum there is an Italian three-barrelled flint-lock pistol of the latter end of the seventeenth century. In this pistol the three barrels turn round upon one common axis, and are brought opposite the flashpan by the hand.

The pistol is well made and by an ingenious contrivance the hammer locks the barrels while in the act of cocking.

The earliest actual revolver was the well-known " pepper-box," a muzzle loader with six barrels in one piece. It was a percussion cap weapon and is particularly interesting because it was " double-actioned," that is to say, pulling the trigger rotated the barrels, cocked and fired it. These pistols were made about 1814 for the first time and a few years later the gunsmith Collier had adopted a spring to revolve the chambers in his pattern.

The single acting principle, in which the chambers are rotated by pulling back the hammer, the trigger being used only for firing purposes, is at

55

least as old as the time of Charles I, and Samuel Colt, who is generally held to be the " father " of the modern revolver, was probably, like so many so-called inventors, little more than an adapter of many notions that had sprung from the brains of those who had gone before him.

Colt's patent, dated 1835, lays particular stress on putting cap nipples in the centre of the chambers and on details of the working of the lock, and these things were doubtless the fruit of his own genius.

The story of Colt's having made his first model with the aid of a pocket knife, from wood, when he was little more than a boy, is probably nothing more than a " story," though there is an old wooden pattern in the Colt factory which is said to be the real, original " Colt." The date is put at 1830, when Colt would have been about sixteen.

Colt was, without doubt, a youngster of more than ordinary ability, for between the ages of 18 and 21 he was touring the United States and Canada as " Dr. Coult," giving a lecture on " Laughing Gas." These lectures won him sufficient money to come to Europe and take out patents for his ideas.

To Messrs. Smith and Wesson belongs the honour of first adapting the revolver to use metallic cartridges. These were rim-fire cases. Pin-fire revolvers were developed in France.

In the early types of Colt pistols the chambers were loaded from the front end by means of a powerful rammer. The bullet had to be a very tight fit to prevent the flash from one chamber firing the charge in the others, which it was apt to do if the bullet was at all loose. Also, if the bullet was loose it was very likely to fall out of the chamber. When metallic cases were first used the rammer was retained to push out the fired cases.

Efficient extraction was a difficulty for a long time. Two schemes were adopted. One made use of the " break-down " principle, similar to that of a shot-gun. This was first adopted by Smith and Wesson, but was considerably improved upon by P. Webley and Son, the forerunners of the well-known Webley and Scott firm.

The Webley pattern had the merit of being " one-handed," so that a horseman could open the weapon and extract the case without leaving his reins.

The other method, which was that of the Colt, used the swinging out of the chambers from the frame to give the necessary force for extraction. This has the merit that the frame can be made in one piece and no top latching is required. Both systems have their admirers amongst practical revolver shots.

In the early days of the revolver, one of the chief difficulties which had to be overcome was the escape of gas between the revolving chambers and the barrel. This difficulty was not lessened by the demand for self-extracting hand-guns, i.e., those in which all the spent cases were ejected in one operation.

Bad escapes of gas at the breech can burn the hand quite severely. It was not until about 1890 that this difficulty was overcome. By this time there were two really good revolvers being manufactured for Service purposes. They were the Webley in England and the Smith-Wesson in America.

The first self-extracting revolver issued to the British Army was made at Enfield and had a .442 inch calibre and rim-fire cartridge. The calibre was enlarged to .450 and a centre-fire cartridge made for the Enfield revolver a few years later. The Webley was adopted as a Service arm in 1890. This revolver was continually improved until it was replaced by the Enfield .38 inch.

It may be thought remarkable that whilst all other Powers are using the automatic pistol, this country should stick to the revolver. This is due to the experience of 1914-18 when the revolver was found to be much more reliable than any make of self-loading pistol. Recent improvement in the pistols have not altered this considered opinion.

The self-loader is superior to the revolver in certain respects. It can fire seven or eight rounds without reloading as against six for the revolver, it can be reloaded more quickly, provided a supply of loaded magazines is available, and it is more convenient to carry. When these things have been said all the advantages of the self-loader have been named.

In the question of reliability the revolver comes out with flying colours and the more severe the comparative tests the better showing the revolver makes.

A defective cartridge resulting in a misfire must be cleared by hand from the self-loader, but with the revolver a fresh cartridge is available by the mere action of pulling the trigger again. The self-loader is liable to any number of temporary and permanent breakdowns. Unburnt grains of powder are likely to clog it and sand and mud quickly put it out of action. The Service Webley and the Enfield .38 are immune from all these troubles.

Finally, though in theory the self-loading pistol should be easier to fire accurately than is the revolver, in practice it is found that the recoil action which ejects the spent case and brings another cartridge into position is very disturbing to the aim.

The first known reference to an automatic pistol appears in the history of the Royal Society, to which, about 1664, that fine soldier and ingenious experimenter, Prince Rupert, reported that a " rare mechanician " had shown him the design of a pistol which, from the description given, was undoubtedly a self-loader. Nothing more was heard of such an idea for about two hundred years, and nothing practical emerged until towards the end of the nineteenth century when a self-loading pistol, the Borchardt, was produced in Germany. It was a clumsy and inefficient weapon and its clumsiness, but not all its inefficiency, has been handed on to the modern German Service pistol, the Luger-Parabellum.

A number of other types and systems appeared rapidly, including the Mauser, which is even more clumsy than the Luger.

It was not until an American invented the Browning and sold the patent rights to a Belgian firm that the self-loading system achieved a real success.

The Browning was simple in operation, light in weight and as reliable as such a weapon can be.

In 1903 the rights in this pistol were acquired by the Colt Firearms Company, who used them as the basis of their Colt self-loader.

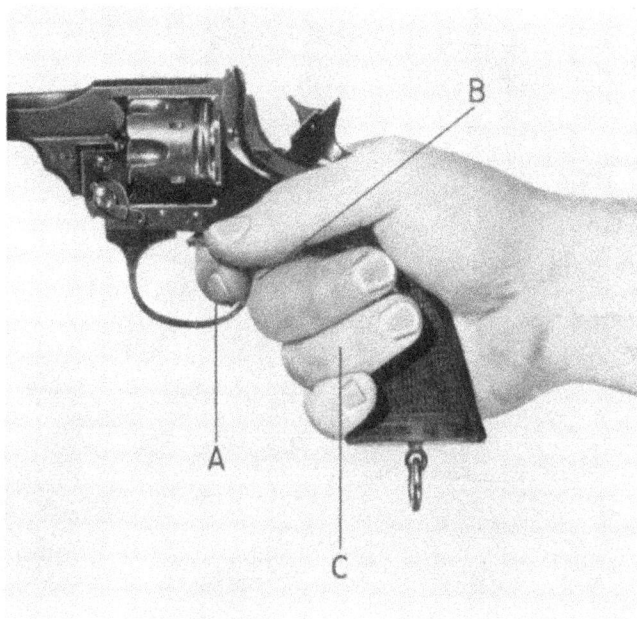

PLATE I.—CORRECT GRIP ON .38 INCH PISTOL BUTT.

A, Index finger comfortably round trigger and low down to give good leverage.   Thumb in position to squeeze against finger pressure.   *B*, Second finger knuckle well up under trigger guard. *C*, Second and third fingers well coiled round butt and pressing it firmly, but lightly, into palm.

61

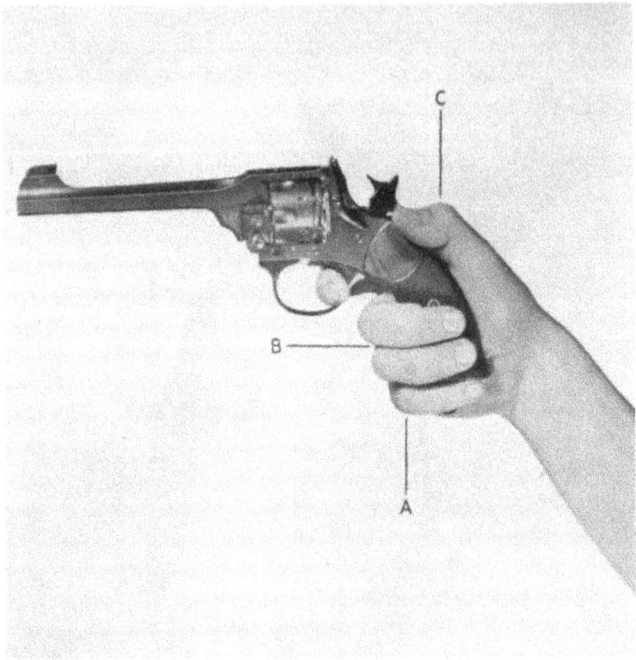

PLATE II.—AN AWFUL EXAMPLE. THE WRONG WAY TO HOLD
THE PISTOL.

A, Little finger under butt. *B*, Second and third fingers trying
to do all the work, and failing. *C*, Thumb not exerting any
pressure.

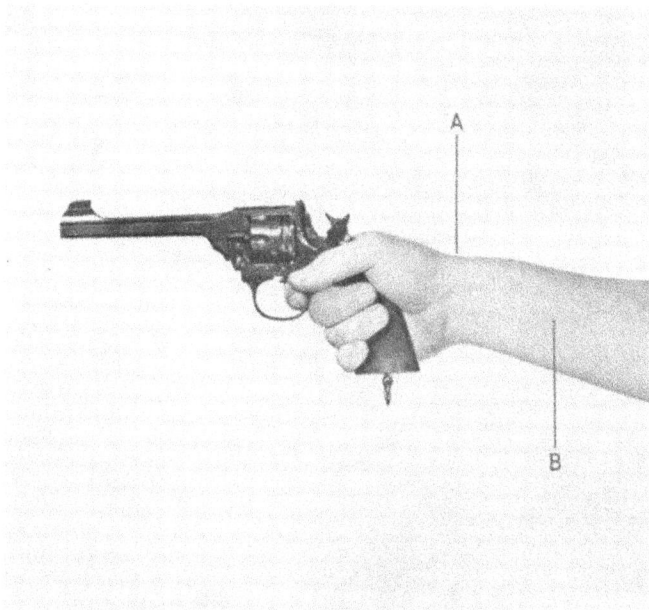

PLATE III.—CORRECT GRIP, SHOWING *A* RIGID WRIST, AND *B* STRAIGHT FOREARM, TO RESIST RECOIL.

PLATE IV.—AIM USING SIGHTS CONSCIOUSLY.

First practise with mirror or instructor. Note straight arm and that butt is wholly enclosed in the hand. Pistol, hand and arm are " one mechanism."

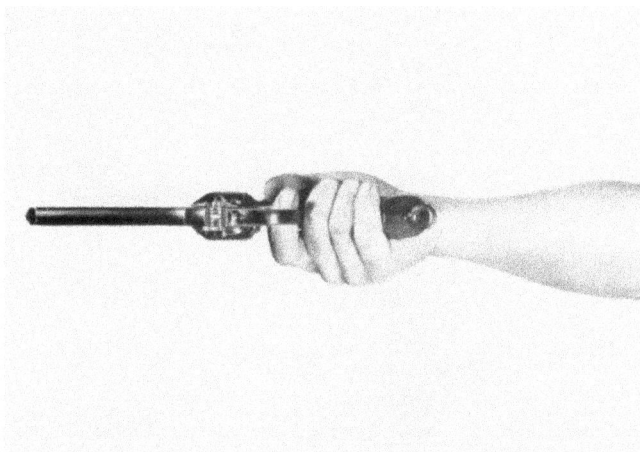

PLATE V.—THE GRIP AND STRAIGHT ARM SEEN FROM BENEATH.
Note position of fingers, particularly trigger finger, and thumb.

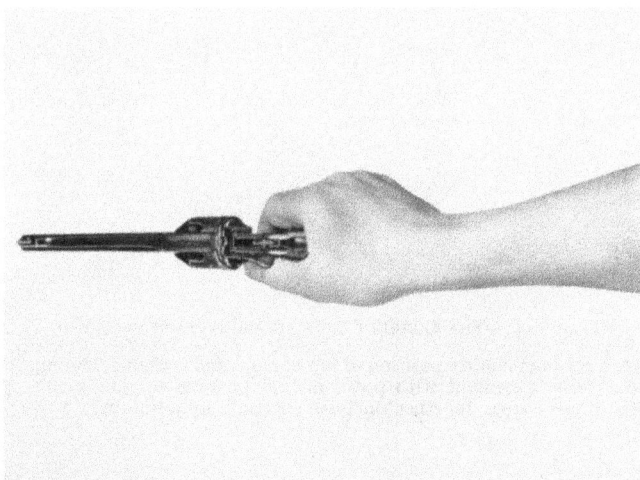

PLATE VI.—THE GRIP AND STRAIGHT ARM SEEN FROM ABOVE.
Note particularly the position of the butt with regard to the
crutch of the thumb.

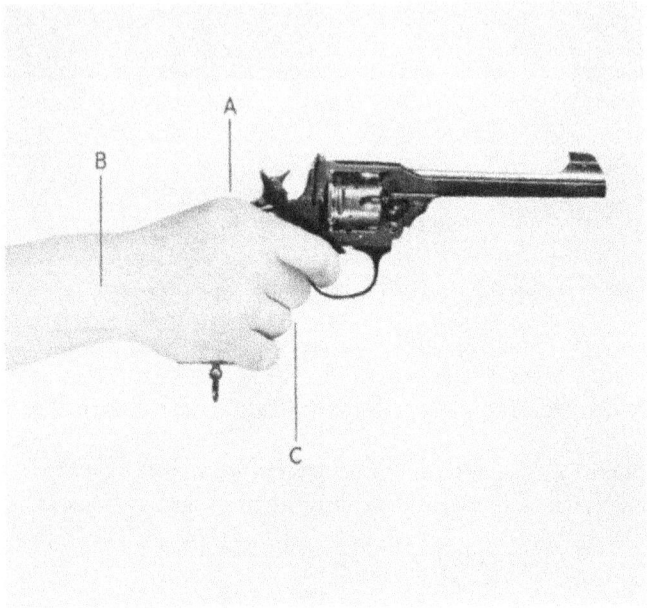

PLATE VII.—THE CORRECT GRIP SHOWING BACK OF HAND.

A, Note particularly position of top of hand and crutch of thumb.
B, Wrist is straight with pistol in best position to take recoil.
C, Fingers close together on butt exerting light but firm grip.

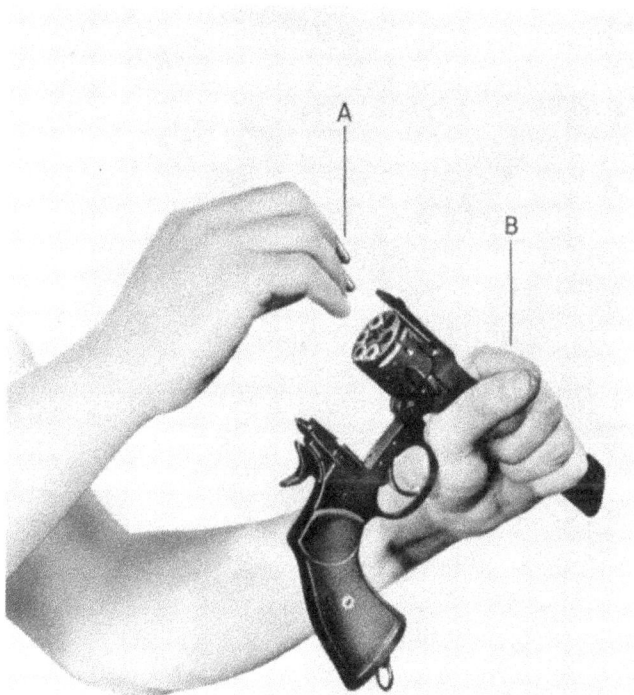

PLATE VIII.—LOADING.

A, Two cartridges gripped together in fingers in correct position
to slip into chambers. *B*, Correct hold. Muzzle pointing downwards at about 45° and to the ground about 3 feet in front of
firer, in direction of target.

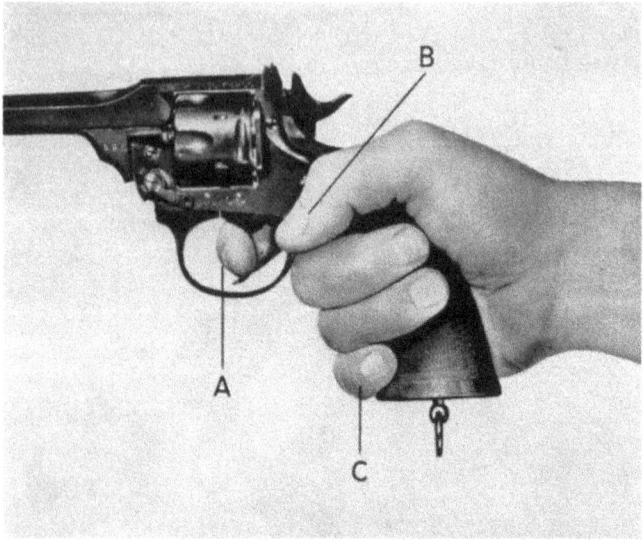

PLATE IX.—DOUBLE ACTION.

Four shots rapid have been fired. Note, comparing with
Plate I, slight shift of grip. *A*, Finger has ridden up on trigger
in taking full pull. *B*, Thumb has been curled down in endeavour
to restore correct grip. Third and little fingers not curled fully
round butt owing to shifting of grip against palm.

•22 Practice with your own •38 Revolver (see page 4)

PARKER-HALE SIX SHOT ADAPTERS.

These are available for the ·38 Enfield Revolver and also ·455 Webley model. They consist of an auxiliary Parkerifled barrel and a new cylinder to take the ·22 Rim-Fire Cartridge. Conversion is quite simple, carried out in a few moments, and does not harm the weapon in any way. Accuracy is fully maintained and we guarantee them to group six shots inside $\frac{3}{4}''$ circle at 20 yards. In the case of the ·38 model it is necessary to send the Revolver to us in order to secure first-class functioning. Price **45/-.**

Read all about this in our Service Catalogue.

BISLEY WORKS   **BIRMINGHAM, 4**

www.ingramcontent.com/pod-product-compliance
Lightning Source LLC
Chambersburg PA
CBHW071419040426
42445CB00012BA/1215